LAUGH
OUT L
ANIM

Uh-oh.

By Jeffrey Burton

LITTLE SIMON
New York London Toronto Sydney New Delhi

LITTLE SIMON

An imprint of Simon & Schuster Children's Publishing Division
1230 Avenue of the Americas, New York, New York 10020
First Little Simon edition April 2017
For information about special discounts for bulk purchases, please contact Simon & Schuster Special Sales at
1-866-506-1949 or business@simonandschuster.com.
The Simon & Schuster Speakers Bureau can bring authors to your live event. For more information or to book an event
contact the Simon & Schuster Speakers Bureau at 1-866-248-3049 or visit our website at www.simonspeakers.com.
Designed by Brittany Naundorff
Manufactured in China 0217 QUL
10 9 8 7 6 5 4 3 2 1
ISBN 978-1-4814-8117-5 (pbk)
ISBN 978-1-4814-8118-2 (eBook)

Welcome and get ready to LAUGH OUT LOUD
with this **Animal Meme Joke Book** that's out to prove once
and for all that wildlife are the funniest critters on earth.

Before you start, here are some helpful tips to make this
book even funnier:

• give each animal its own special voice
• give each joke its own special delivery
• make sure you share the best jokes with your friends
• and don't be afraid to make up your own jokes, too!

MONKEY FACT:

The one who smelt it, *dealt it.*

BOB'S FINALLY COMING OUT OF HIS SHELL.

Excuse me.

you gonna EAT that?

WHO YOU CALLIN'

CHEETAHS?!

Picture day did not go well
for Little Kitty Paws.

ZEE

HA

How
zebras
laugh:

BRAH-HA-HA! HA-HA-HA! HAHA-HA-HA-HA HA-HA-HA-HA HAHA-HAHA-HA-HA! HAHA-HA-HA-HA!

MY PEOPLE NEED ME.

POLLY REALLY WANTED A CRACKER.

IS IT A LITTLE FROGGY OUT?
OR IS IT JUST ME?

CHEESE BOOGERS

All I said was "Red's not your color!"

Gnarly airwalk, Tiny Turtle!

Look **deep** into my eyes . . .

you are getting very sleeeeepy.

This was a fuR ReaL bad idea....

Rhino what to do ...

JUMP!

SLOOOOOW and

STEADY

wins

the ...

DRAMATIC. PENGUIN.
SLO-MO. WALK.

IGUANA
MAKE YOU LAUGH

HORSE CHEESE

Talk to me
I'M ALL EARS

AM I COOL YET?

SHH . . .
I'M HIDING

IF I FITS, I SITS.

HOO HOO HOO

you talkin' to?

I CAN'T OPEN IT!

You're a **slippery** one, Tweeters.

I CAN SEE YOU

MONKEY FACT:
it hurts when I do this.

(Don't do that.)

DID YOU SAY CAR RIDE?!

THE MOUSEHAT WAS
NOT STEVE'S STYLE.

STEVE, YOUR HAT IS FREAKING ME-OWT.

Raise your hand
if you ate too much
honey!

Meow you see me,

meow you don't!

THE FISH WAS

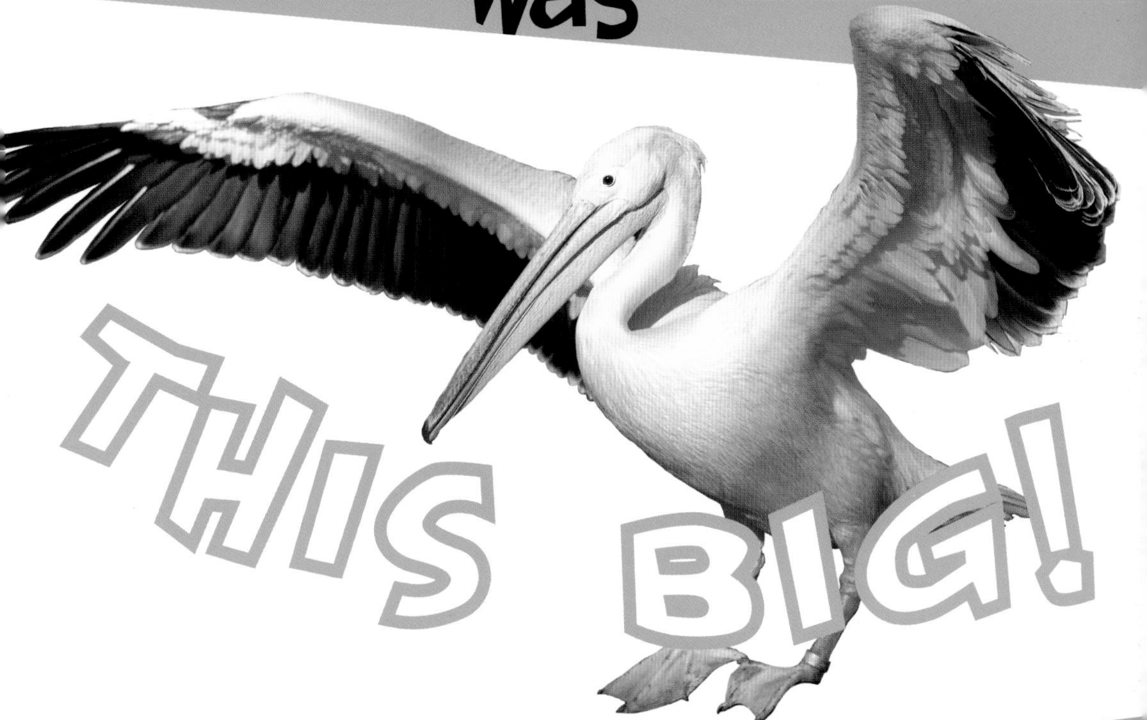

THIS BIG!

I SWEAR!

Grandma sent me another sweater...

the dog party was

OFF THE LEASH!

When you realize there's

on Monday.

Are you

KID-DING

me?

YOUR MOVE, HUMAN.

Fred caught the UFO and saved all dog-kind.

**WHEN MOM COMBS
YOUR HAIR**

THE
SHOW
MUST
GO
PAW-N

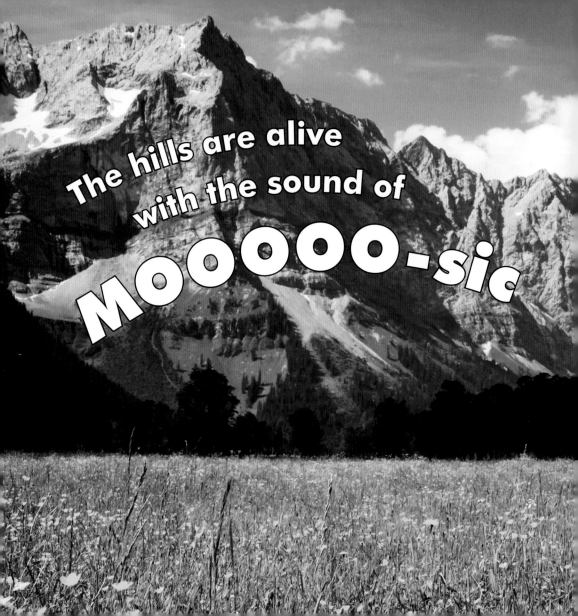

I MEAN BUSINESS

MONKEY BUSINESS

LLAMA DRAMA!

ALL NINE LIVES FLASHED BEFORE WHISKERS' EYES.

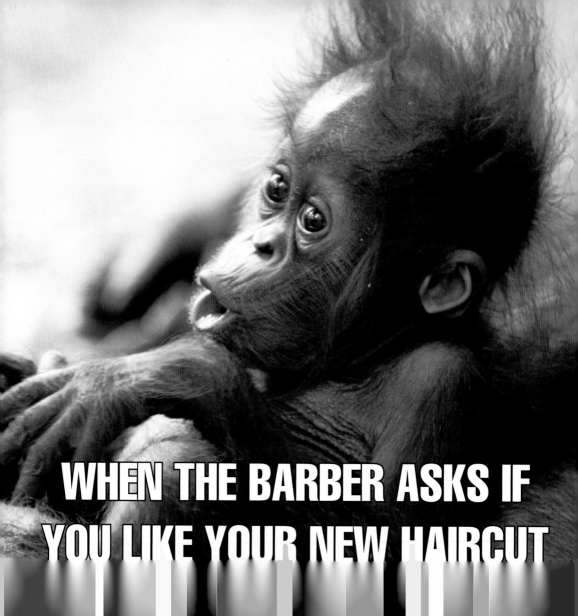

WHEN THE BARBER ASKS IF YOU LIKE YOUR NEW HAIRCUT

Soooooooo tired . . .

Only slept for 21 hours.

YOU'RE WEARING *THAT* AGAIN?

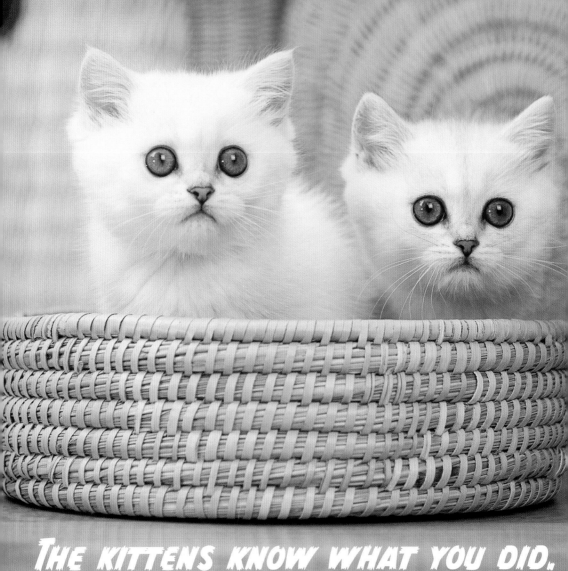

THE KITTENS KNOW WHAT YOU DID.

COWABUNGA, DUDE!

JUST SAY NO
to yellow
snow.

I am definitely **NOT** a flying squirrel.

AND THEN SHE PUT THE DOG IN TIME-OUT!

BOW-WOW DOWN
TO YOUR KING AND QUEEN.

This flower **stinks.**

Talk
to the
PAW

MOM!!!
I CAN'T FIND
MY SHOES!!

The dancing
lemur waits
for no one.

CHA-CHA-CHA!

I'm afraid it's bad news...
You're a cat.

MY HUGS ARE THE

BEST KOALA-TY

My lips are
SEALED

So this is the other side? Boring!

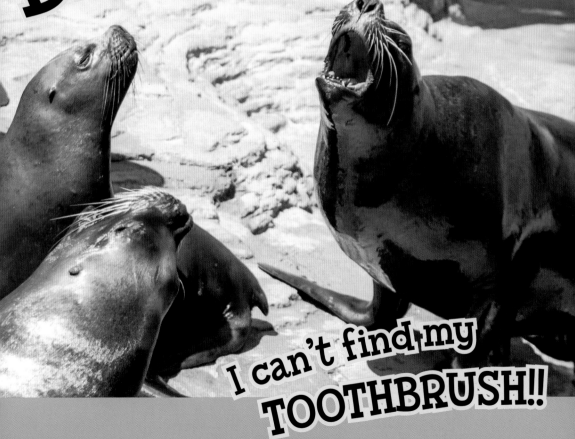

THE BIRDS. THEY TEASE ME.

DON'T LOOK!
(I'm neigh-ked!)

DEEP IN HIS BURROW,

FURBALL PLOTS HIS REVENGE.

NO
SCHOOL
TODAY!!

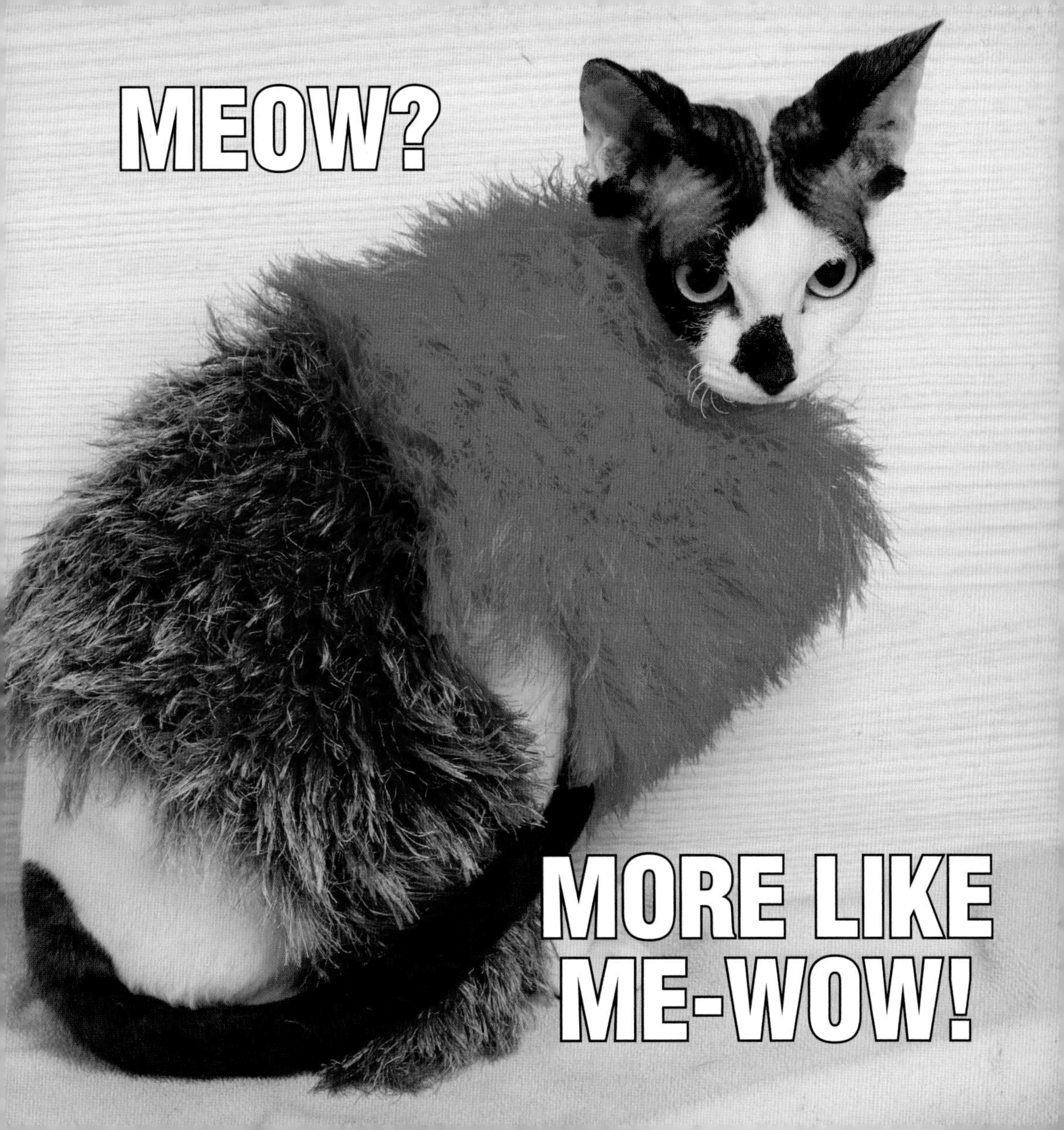
MEOW?
MORE LIKE
ME-WOW!

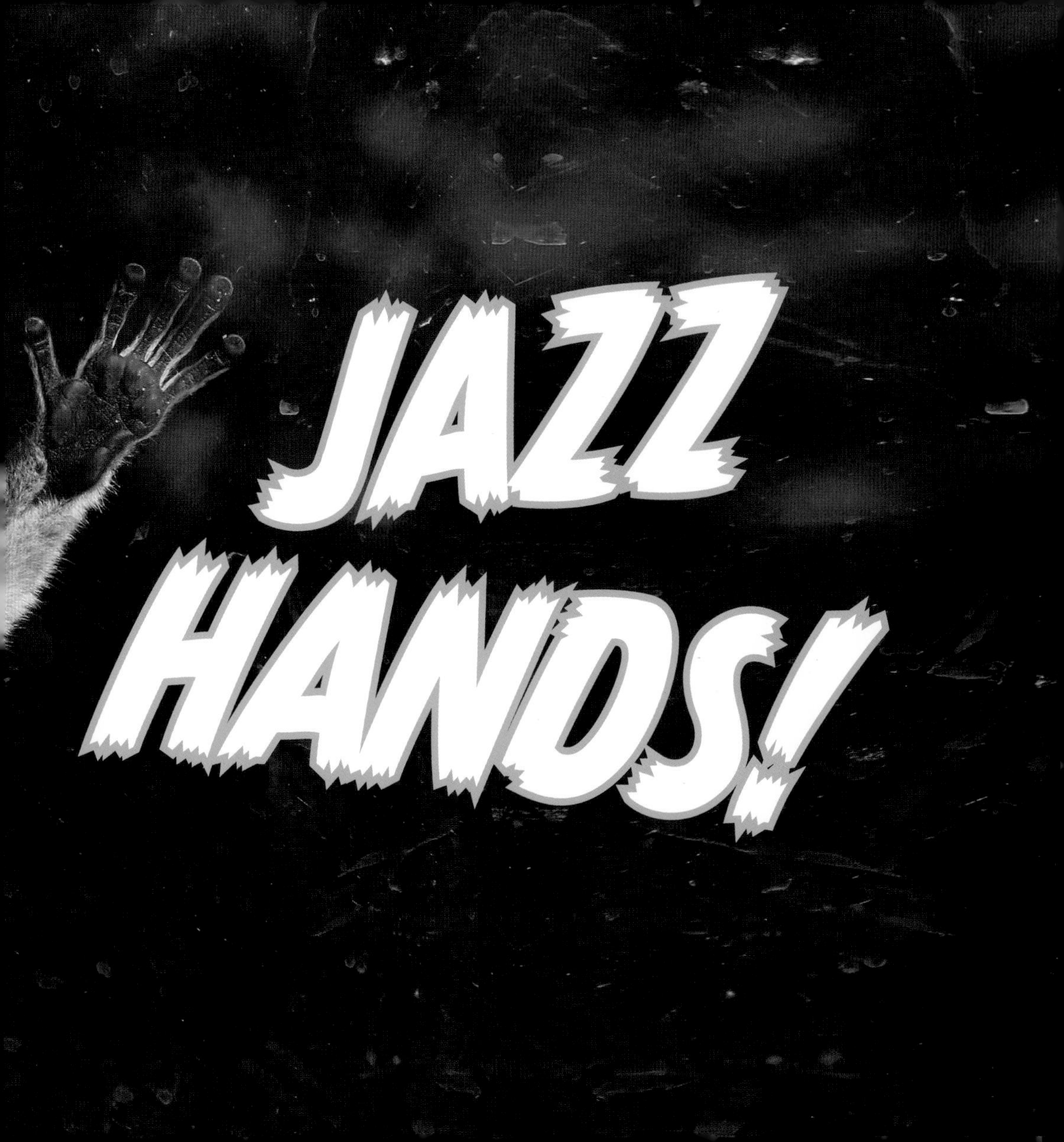
JAZZ
HANDS!

GOT ME LIKE ...

Homework is for the

BIRDS

TREE-HUGGER.

I ATE THE Easter Bunny

Just wait,
I'm going to be a

Beautiful
Batterfly

Drool-free guarantee!

Welcome to

DOGSMART

POOP OR TREAT

CAN YOU HANDLE THE PUG LIFE?

HOVER PUPPY!

POLAR BROS

4 LIFE!

I'm not
DONNER,

I'm BLiTZEN

THE KOALA KNOWS WHAT YOU DID.

THE CAT DID IT.

I LEFT YOU A PRESENT.

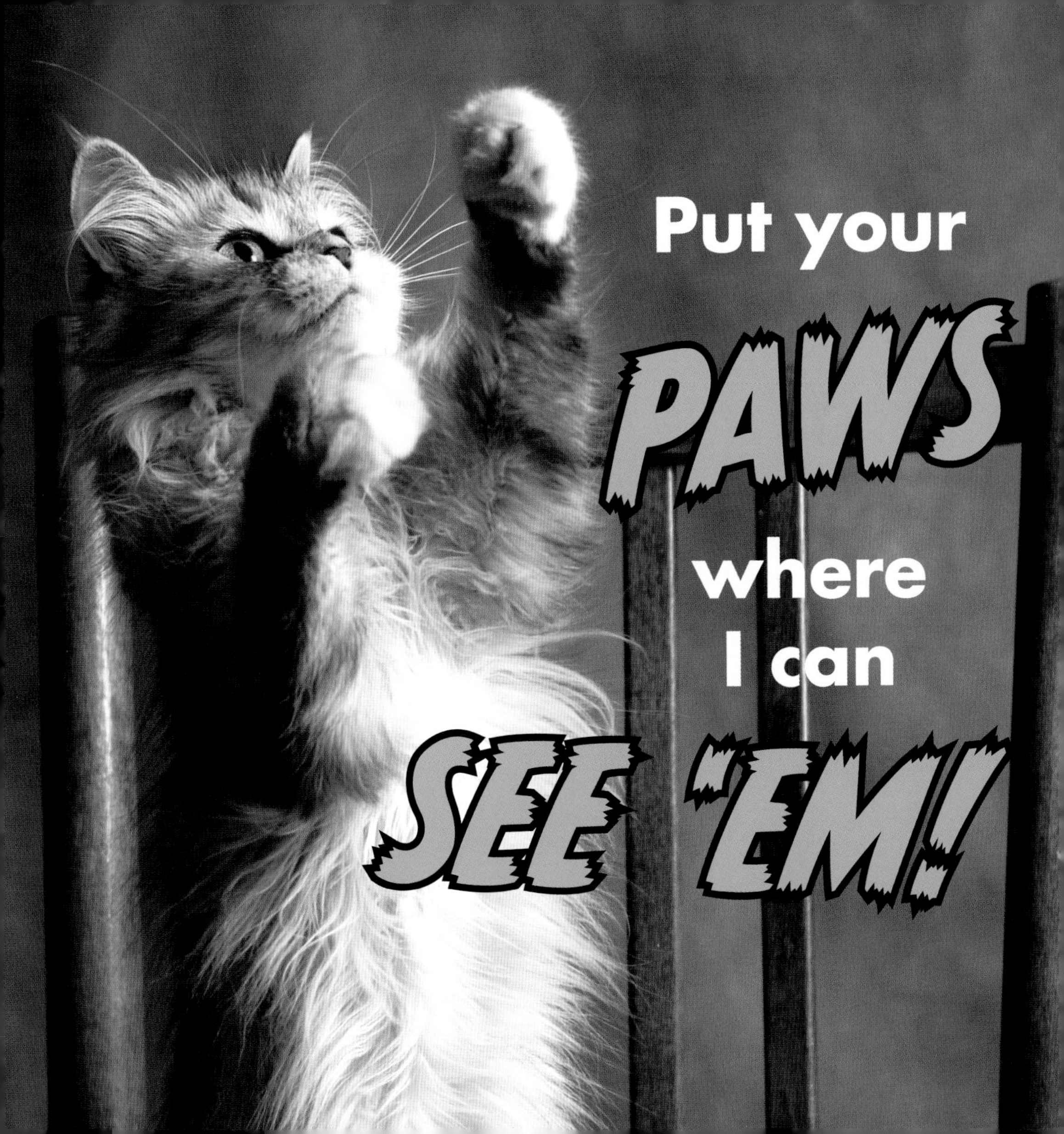
Put your
PAWS
where
I can
SEE 'EM!

UP! UP!

And away!

BET WE LOOK
AWESOME
DOING THIS
SYNCHRONIZED
SWIMMING THING,
LARRY.

TONIGHT, WE FEAST.

THAT JOKE WAS UNBEARABLE.

UHHH... I THINK I PUMA PANTS....

OH NO SHE DI-IN'T.

It's a bird!   It's a plane!

IT'S A
BAAAA

WHO ARE YOU CALLIN' CHICKEN?

I like to knit.

KING PUPPY
REQUIRES A BONE.

DACHSHUND
THROUGH THE SNOW...

HOW COME THE MOUSE NEVER CHASES ME?

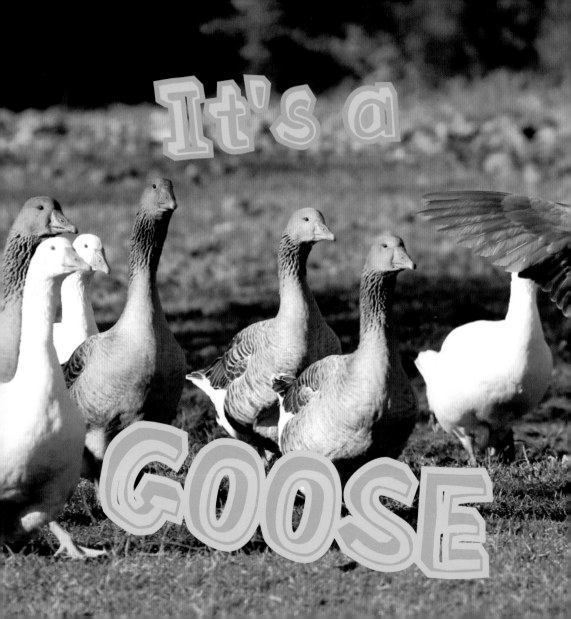

It's a
GOOSE

IT'S RAINING CATS AND DOGS?

That sounds terrible.

HOW'S THIS FOR BREAKING THE ICE?

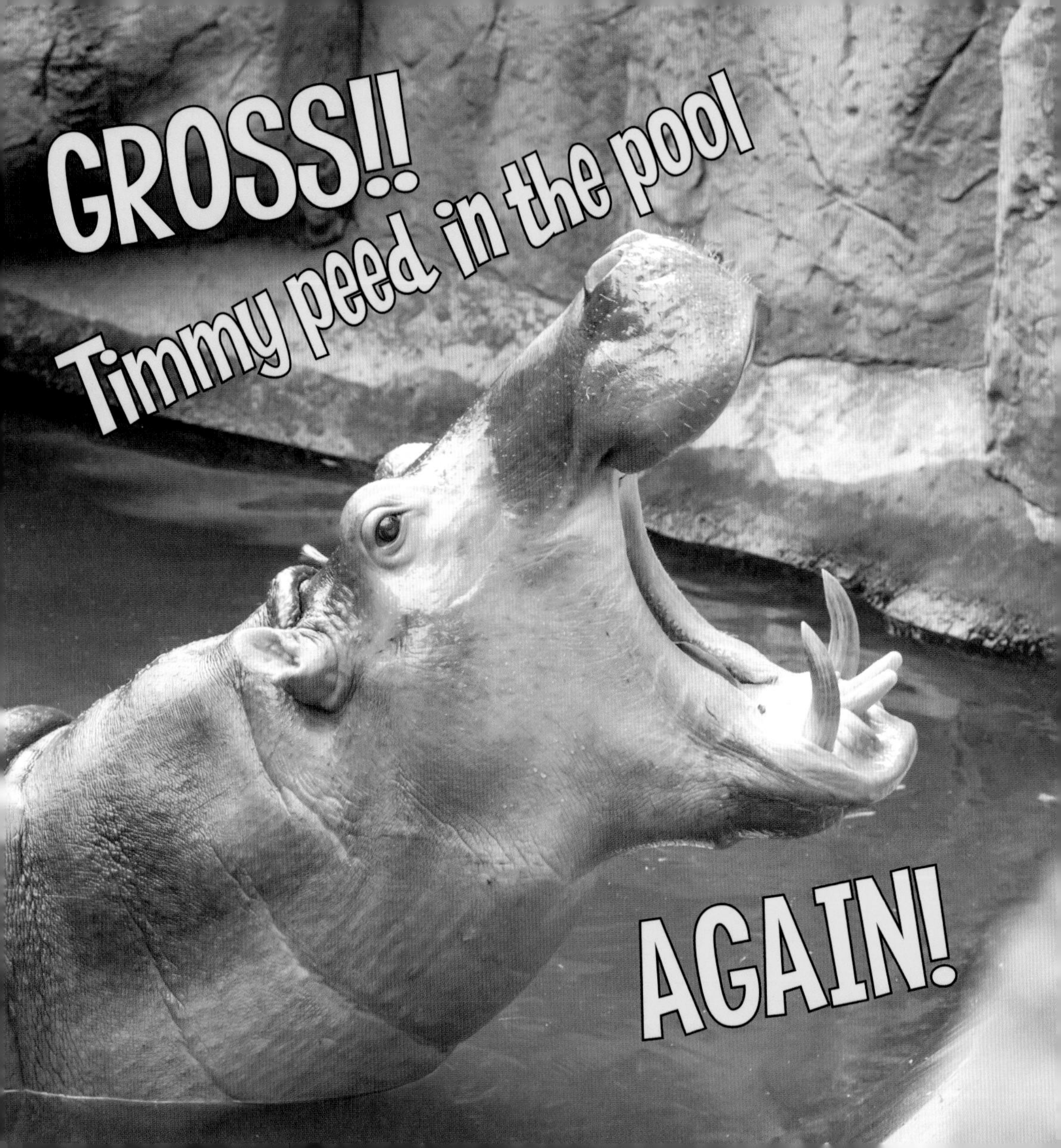
GROSS!!
Timmy peed in the pool
AGAIN!

for you, my love.

Meow YOU doin'?